TRESPASS

THE NATIONAL POETRY SERIES

The *National Poetry Series* was established in 1978 to ensure the publication of five poetry books annually through five participating publishers. Publication is funded by the Lannan Foundation; Stephen Graham; Joyce & Seward Johnson Foundation; Juliet Lea Hillman Simonds; The Poetry Foundation; and Olafur Olafsson.

2013 COMPETITION WINNERS

Ampersand Revisited, by Simeon Berry of Somerville, MA
Chosen by Ariana Reines,
to be published by Fence Books

Bone Map, by Sara Eliza Johnson of Salt Lake City, UT
Chosen by Martha Collins,
to be published by Milkweed Editions

Its Day Being Gone, by Rose McLarney of Tulsa, OK
Chosen by Robert Wrigley,
to be published by Penguin Books

What Ridiculous Things We Could Ask of Each Other,
by Jeffrey Schultz of Los Angeles, CA
Chosen by Kevin Young,
to be published by University of Georgia Press

Trespass, by Thomas Dooley of New York, NY
Chosen by Charlie Smith,
to be published by HarperCollins Publishers

TRESPASS

POEMS

Thomas Dooley

HARPER  PERENNIAL

NEW YORK • LONDON • TORONTO • SYDNEY • NEW DELHI • AUCKLAND

HARPER PERENNIAL

HarperCollins books may be purchased for educational, business, or sales promotional use. For information, please e-mail the Special Markets Department at SPsales@harpercollins.com.

FIRST EDITION

Designed by Fritz Metsch

Library of Congress Cataloging-in-Publication Data has been applied for.

ISBN 978-0-06-233882-2

14 15 16 17 18   OV/RRD   10 9 8 7 6 5 4 3 2 1

For my mother and my father

Contents

TRESPASS

CHERRY TREE

My father
mows tight squares
around her, she

rains pink on him
a rock

cracks inside the blades
she beats down
flurries

I've grown
too lush

don't leave me
with him

PART ONE

INGALLS AVENUE

the house lit of blue television of snow
the house where my father got tall
house of sturdy pipes house a home
for his sisters house of winter
boots and calico and wooden
spoons house of my grandfather
his girls grandkids house of quiet
sheer things of vinyl shingles
the padding around the house
the house of bins of old clothes and moon
light open windows of gulping
curtains the house of dusty aster
the house of women once girls a house
of kisses this is a house of rooms
a house of small closets and
smaller closets a closet for lemon
candy tucked back a closet
of cedar panels of tongue
and groove of bulbs a closet for small
things for tall things a closet for slumped
tall things and small things this
is a closet for tall and small things

Eastern Red Cedars

I walk by your fragrant bodies
thinned by winter,   your young ones

are burlapped in nurseries, some are planked,
chipped-up
        seamed for chests & trunks:

inside a cedar closet, my father at sixteen

        one bulb setting

your rose panels aflame, his lit face
the white heart, his narrow body, wick,

his niece, four years old

        his head knocks the light   his hand
        steadies the wild
        string

the light

eclipsed, then bright

CEDAR CLOSET, 1955

He is sixteen and takes her
inside, jars
the unquiet hinge

she waits

forty years to name
him, Aunt Peggy says

you might as well be dead.

And now

it's spring. My father's hair
thins, dull moth-gray, the last

clouds sink like sacks, the trees
are wet, sweat
on a body, damp wool.

MY FATHER AS A BOY

his arm is the smallest to snake
the toilet's trapway, at night

a body can vanish
in the dark house, under covers I see

his smallness, a sharp elbow, remember
my smallness as he gathered my body in bed

he wakes to his sister
and father at the foot of the bed

his father kissing her neck
hands running up her night blouse

fingertips treading to a clasp
sliding a hook from its eye

LATE BLOOMER

at sixteen
my father stood
at the full-length
mirror naked and
touched
his chest
his hairless
legs touched
between them
he told me once
he thought his body
was small
and quiet
like a girl's

Hunger

We sat scissor-legged on the carpet
popped open the suitcase, a storm of tulle

she pulled Barbie
from the waves

caftan made from a pocket square
she showed me to drag

blond hair through
dryer sheets to tame the wisps

she stopped my hand
stuck on the brush stuck in knots

here the spray for tangles
I crossed the hallway

to her brother's room
he took off

my corduroy shorts, took off
his wildlife tee

against a polar sky
the airbrushed wolves

ORDINARY TIME

In the sacristy my father
rinsed cruets smothered wicks

the monsignor pulled off
a chasuble of emerald silk

moved his hands
down my father

the choir shook
handbells from the loft

what my father did
when he moved

to her body when he lifted
her green dress

Maybe in an Atlas

Maybe another New Jersey
somewhere. Linden wood
as cash cow. And a way out. If my father grew
taller that year, sudden. Reached
the high altar wicks, a Moses
in Egypt. Bigger than the priests. What if deus
ex machina. Or a catcher.
No rye. Rye watered
down. Rocks to mean rocks. Not
glacial. Not a cold hand
anywhere. A siren sounds
on skin. Maybe a pie
in the window. Adults made big gestures
with giant hands. He wasn't soft.
Boney, but not folded
like egg whites, hankies.
In his yearbook: "Aspiration: farmer."
Tall as corn, as noon sun. Only if he grew
taller, sudden, he wouldn't be
lightweight linden, maybe a hundred
proof. She was proof. Girls
were softer. Maybe his hand
looked giant. And she lay down
softly. Like he was made to, maybe.

FIRST LOVE

At the bar last night
I couldn't believe it was you
standing by the men in leather collars
your layman's jeans and work boots
the same tough suede I remember
below your vestment's hem
at altar boy camp, tea lights
in our cabin, I always hoped
you would choose me
to start the flames.
Now you travel the decade
of my spine, your mouth sudden
on each bone, I turn you over
my lips drag heat
from the thin chaplet of hair
shrining your navel, I hold you
like a chaperone at a theme park
when you held me as we looped
through air and at Mass
when you placed in my hand
a body I could eat.

I Saw You Once

on a Brooklyn corner, fronds
of palm, your sachet
of lemon halves, you ask
if I'm Jewish, how we
look like brothers—
jet hair, same skin
a tincture of chickpeas,
our noses not Roman
nor button, I want to appeal:
let me celebrate with you. Listen, my voice
can match the glottal timbre
of your prayers, let me unfurl the black
curls by your ears like scrolls, read
your thoughts, your oils fragrant
on my fingertips.

A Body Glows Bronze

the Belgian soldier
his uniform slung

over a chair back
creases preserved

a man with war
in him yet

retreats under
a studio lamp

his dense sinew
muscled how

a body glows
bronze under your rub

the artist's knife
his clay-tipped fingers

the soldier's blazer
in the corner

late sun sets
fire to brass buttons

LATE BLOOMER

Spindle-heart at fourteen,
and eighty-five pounds. But you had

a dusting of hair above your lip, dark stains
under your arms after relays.

White-primed, gessoed canvas, I felt untouched,
untouchable, gilt icon in plexi, I wanted

your size, a potency,
yeast that balloons.

Still I was
unleavened and wafer-thin.

Brunch

Cold tea bag pressed
in a napkin, my father

picks at toast.

Bobby, his sister says
there are some accusations

against you,

your niece, well,

she goes
to a therapist,

he tells her to

shit on
your photo.

My mother runs
to the kitchen and vomits
in the sink.

He leans
over cold
eggs, what's left on the plate

my mother comes back
a damp cloth

to her mouth
she moves

clutching
the tall chair backs

breathes in to slide
behind his chair, it's quiet

on Mildred Avenue, brakes
scream down Ingalls

my mother clears her plate
reaches for his.

Snapshot

Her therapist said find one put it
on the bathroom floor so she searched albums
for his face the picnic photos
at the grill his head smoke-capped limp hands
fanning charcoal then her wedding proofs
all the uncles in suits and one close-up
my father bow-tied tipped black
seesaw at his throat open smile
his tongue a small peak he's calling to someone
outside the frame his right hand bent
in mid gesture his fingernails a bit long
and in focus the tips the whitest

SCREENSHOT

I watch the clip
of you moved

to pleasure, freeze
on white pixels

my hand rolls down
a slow storm

I move with your
thunder, we are twinned

rhythms, the joy
you shake from me

TRANSFERENCE

I was working
in the theater's toolroom
when my father called
Mom told me
about your new
friend and I thought
you can't even
say it and I squeezed
a pair of pliers in my hand
as the paint sink kicked back gunk
and hung up the phone
hung up the pliers
aligning their jaws.
In the wings it was dark
I instructed the actor
playing a waiter
how to wring
the grinder, crack
whole corns
to coarse pepper.

In That Light

he was all angles
L of jaw, shoulders a ledge

of granite, I thought
he seemed biblical

the perfection of the tribes
settling into his thunder
                              thick honeyed wrists
and I was yielding,
of linen.

Darwin would study his dense
bicuspids, long feet hitting

the earth, his cock
slapping thighs, he needs

me to praise him
he needs men

to tell him, or show him
or show on him when

that weekend in July
on the sandy cape that hooks a bay
the salt a skin on him, moonlight
violent with silver on him

the other man's
bright tongue

how strangers can validate
how that man knelt to him

and he comes home to me

Sperm Donor

And then
a hatch
      threw open

a flush of blood, pink-
cheeked,

you broadcast:
They want my sperm!

You imagine your stuff
flying through tangle
bursting to a field
a privet of XYs—
flourish little ones!

They will spin
and set in that lesbian womb, form
bones, push white elbow and
purple cord into a dark
pixilated frame,

fine
set in them your link

that quiet boat
you send into me
that never finds dock

Away

I pile books on the bed
in your place, calculate

the weight of you, I crowd
the pillows like

bodies, all night I'm wasteful
with lamplight

GUEST ROOM

A bed too short,
our feet slide out

and cup the brass
footboard, cool

in our concaves, what
my father would do

to find us: curled
fiddleheads, one

cochlea intricate
as fist, oil slicked

metallic on pond
our bodies'

edges imbricate, in
the morning we

divide and in a year
we separate.

PART TWO

SEPARATION

I

I want to say something
about sabotage. How you
designed it.

I am scooping dry food
to a deaf cat, no longer

in our kitchen, the old marble
mantle I left
vacant,

remember when greens of spruce
brought indoors
made us suffer the winter less?

II

What hurts
the most?   The kept

breath? Geese
cutting the pond? I came
to know

in hard Texas heat you found

him,

back east the roads twice salted cracked
in places, I played on loop

carols of mystery,

O
magnum mysterium, then
acute ice,

and common rain

III

The sun on the avenue
is bright, veneers

of antique chests at the outdoor flea
shine like chestnut skins,
a gray sparkle lifts
from costume jewelry.

Knowing you are browsing
cheap Swedish furniture
makes me feel,
sturdier?

IV

I want to solder
the fragile things, pour
liquid alloy into me or

exit metaphor
altogether,
        straw is just straw,
not hair,
not blond tin,
it's dull and dirty, grass

is young under straw, breaks
capsules, the shredded
chaff becomes
dirt. I could
be these things.
Dirt.
Shredded.

Nothing seems
degradable. Memory is still
of you—morning, naked, peeling
a small orange over
a silver bowl.

My teeth hurt,
the citrus and the metal.

V

I try to forget you every day
but Lauren and I were discussing
superpowers and she said
she would like to have super strength,
I thought I'd like teleportation
but then thought telepathy—to read
your mind—but Lauren said ignorance
is bliss, I had to agree. We thought
Spiderman had it right with scaling walls
which made me think of Luc in Aix
who climbed building façades for sport,
often shirtless, Lauren thought
that was super strength but I said no it's more like
super attachment and I saw the power
I kept giving you.

VI

I see you as a boy
at the community garden
lacing tomato stems, your hands
quick with twine. I watch
the direct daydream
of your stare, how
your green eyes cycle
light. You mind the squash curls
before you race out the gate
shoelaces wild on the pavement
snap like jacks.

VII

You say you need
time yet I keep
coming back
isn't my heart
the dumbest kid
in the class
the dirty kid who
no one wants
to sit next to but he
reaches out with gum
and granola bars and
they scratch into his desk
with the needle
from a math compass
they ink "THINK SOAP"
on the beige enamel of his locker
he doesn't know
anything better just
days when Xander
is absent and the room
falls quiet he thinks
in the moments
when chalk scrapes
a music of slate
a sparkle of white
dust it's all radiant theater

this escape might make
him happy that the kids
love him and he
has good lunches
and he swings for hours
upside down from the monkey bars
his head pendulous
just above chipped-up
wood as his shadow
draws giant totems
on the grass shrinking
and growing shrinking
and growing for hours
he could do that
as blood charges his head
and he feels
he might pass out
from the wild joy
he is a bell clanging
as if to call everyone
and shout this is all
my body can do
up this high
you can't touch me
as long as I keep pumping
my skinny arms.

VIII

Chestnuts harden in spiky
green husks, my brothers and I

would walk the driveway
in our socks, braved it

under the chestnut tree
and you give me

a husk to hold
suffer its unkindness.

IX

It's been five weeks
since I left you and I leave

the family brunch, pass
the hidden plastic eggs.

Today the tomb
is not empty, the stone

still wedged in. I can't go on
distracting myself

from the smell
of burial spices

the disturbed earth, you
have not come back.

X

Fridays are the hardest.
Your body moves through
happy hours without
me, I can't even
chart you,
            I want
to see the lines
you make
on the map of the city,
if they cross the lines
I make, do we
create a pattern
unknowingly,
            does my finger
run down the glass
at the table you just left
at the café on Dekalb? We are
no longer destinations,
single blinking dots.

XI

If I forget, remind me
when we drove

past the dry roadside
farms, remind me when I looked out

on the neat
wheels of hay, my breathing

hard then stilled, what you never said
when I wiped my face,

remind me of your
neglect and the long ditches

and if I forget the annulling
of the day, if I want a night

with you, let that car ride
remind me.

XII

Our first time back together,
magnets, my body

pushed into you and your eyes
rolled back. The second time

I stared at your feet
while I sucked you off

the small muscles
in my calves squeezed

and released.
The heart?

The first position of union, the second
something polar,

getting back to your place
that first time

was like flight. The second,
traffic at the bridge—as if the city

said *wait here*
don't cross the water.

XIII

here take a universe   darts of light   a pan flute
chirps our ending song   go now to the cedary wield of smooth
creatures   of glabrous torsos caprine legs   who am I
to clasp seedstorms barehanded   mornings when the surf
clung to its mist   stubborn   I will make this break soft as skiff
on water   gone in a sprint you sleek windjammer   I give you
June's tea rose heat   island's sagebrush   summer and young trees

XIV

On the radio, bombast
of timpani and horn
from the Slovak Symphony, you are

nowhere in the glissando
the piccolo is
too bright
for you

in these passages
of fullness
you do not live

nor on the bridge today
midlake birdsong, glottal frog
that's when I sang
to become hoarse.

XV

this morning water broke
over my shoulders
the shower was ice
the longer I stayed
today is a cold day
longer now after
the solstice more sunlight
and snow I keep you
alive even though I try
to kill you every day

PART THREE

FATHER

he's dulled
my blade

sometimes I could
throw hatchets

look at me
enfeebled pullet

offer my beak

blunt the hooked
end

my air empties, ink
clots

when I think *write*
him

PHONE CALL

Have you
written her?

Many times.

What did you
say?

I asked her to forgive me.

But you don't
have the right
to ask
that.

Why
can't I ask her that?

You don't
have the right.

AUNT PEGGY

Afternoon sun on metals, hubcaps
flash on Second Avenue, I've been
seesawing my feet on the edge of the curb
for almost an hour on the phone
with my mother, *It just doesn't make*
sense, the subject always comes up,
I mean she's had years
of therapy, she says *years* with such
exhalation her breath gets
reedy, I pick threads from my scarf,
Why can't Peggy forgive your father? The city is
bright, winter is quiet, a pause
on motion, *Mom, look at all she's been through, Pop*
then Dad, I mean, good god, her voice
tenders, *But Tom,* she ticks her throat,
don't you think after all that therapy
she would be able to forgive? I can feel
a draft in my sleeve, it hits
the sweat at the bend of my arm, *Maybe this is*
her therapy. Treat Dad like he's dead.
There is a shallow dent in the chrome
fender of an old car my image runs over
and warps, my mother is quiet,
I've handed her something new, she might
stand for a while in her kitchen and wait
for the dishwasher to end its cycle.

PICNIC, 1988

I don't name his niece here
but I know she was there
by the potato salad. In a notebook

I sketched my house
and the giant pines, our front porch
green-black like lake mud

erased until the paper broke, shaded
shingles with new colors, signed
my name bottom right.

I let Aunt Peggy look.
I was young but I knew her life
was sad, she took

in her hands the brittle
sketch, her eyes tracing lines, down
the charcoaled driveway, her eyes

I will name blue, her blue
eyes, those glassy
empty rooms.

WARINANCO PARK

Shadows slide over
the fields, the sun

vanishes I think one black vulture
has eclipsed it, but

no, it's quick clouds, dead leaves
are kites unto the heave.

The planes lift from Newark
crossing over the park,

over the clover leaves
of the 1 and 9, from above, the streets

are pale laces and the roof
of my father's house,

a chip, a tiny smudge
over those living beneath.

Selling the House: Ingalls Avenue

In the sun parlor after dusk
I want to turn the heat
on, the tall lamp is shadeless,

the new tenant knocks
his knuckle to find patches
of new plaster, my father turns keys

over, they chitchat, *I might enclose*
the front porch, make it a bedroom,
there's light on bits of lint.

Another big family to move in, more
quiet pairings, I look out curtainless
windows, in a house with rooms

and closets that never knew to be
unlived in, for this moment maybe
a relief to be empty.

At Windward and Shore Roads

When we sold her house
the pine sent down
its last dried arrows, the new owner
sawed the cherry still in bloom,
that holly that always snagged
her white perm was pieced
and bundled,
                    her new condo
has fresh paint, no mold in the walls, she's far
from the bay where she took me
to push horseshoe crabs
back in, now she hears waves
of engines behind the huge oaks
beyond the parking lot
where the highway runs out.

Winter Burial

When she died, early light
turned the curtains

to gauze. I wilted
spinach for lunch

the hours she spent
zesting lemons

whipping meringue
to peaks. We step

between dunes of ice,
she never

liked snow.
Its weight on a roof.

Elegy

FOR TYLER

I know violin strings

you have to
make them
tremble

     a quick hand against
the steady hill
of your shoulder

in the shallow valley
by your neck
       thresh the horse hairs

of your bow over
the ridge and drag
back,   full

as a field   released

to a hurtling
a long falling
gallop

DYING FAMILY

I

At the church door
its heavy wood
in the treeless lot
I take my father's
hand we move
over the broken rocks
turn their broken
sound we move
within the shadow
the spire makes
on the lawn away
from the door those
slate steps rain-dark
he passes his sisters
seated in cars
headlights on single
file I move my hand
over his back
another funeral
my father's brothers
are dying his sisters
survive and want
him dead.

II

Did you see
when my brother
reached over
and my father
fell into him, hair
silver as winter,
his head
tucking under?
Did you see
the small quake
of his back,
my father's tall
body bend,
a peony
burst open,
top-heavy?

III

My father's niece crosses to me
I kneel to her newborn
I think we're all smiling.

We're moving
to Florham Park, she says.

Florham. That word,
floral
and florescence, lawns

of snow and spring,   a space
opening

blacktop becomes
field, no

manholes of City
of Linden,   I watch

a burst seed drift
and land
in the bed
of her brunette curl, I almost
brush it away.

Never

Did it stop with me?

Yes,
I knew
it was wrong.

She adjusts the strap
to her pocketbook.

Never
to your children?

MEMORY

My brothers and I hunted
night crawlers in summer

folded back the ground
with large dinner spoons the metal

necks bent swans we sunk
our cupped hands below crinolines

of white roots found
quick rubbery coils ruby

under light dropped each
into an empty Sanka can

their wet bodies sliding
away from cold tin

my father says he forgot about
the other two girls.

At dawn the rain fills in
the pocks with mud.

MARY AND BOBBY

My father writes
to his mother who died
when he was four,

I moved out of Linden
and I like the quiet of this new
town. I go to daily Mass.
You would love Carol.

He asks about the scar

large as a map running
down over his elbow,

Did you scream

when you pulled my arm
from between the cylinders
of the clothes wringer?

He pauses
to let her respond
like prayer, he waits

to hear something
come back,

Dear Bobby,

Keep writing
to me. Go teach
good things
to those boys.

You were
only sixteen.

I should have
been there.

St. Gertrude's

iron gates scatter low-flying gulls
    her brother impales an empty can
on a blunt spear-tip   twilight
blanches stones uniformly
    some lindens effloresce
    her brothers stumble to Pop's
grave   it has no new
bouquets   onion
grass shoots up   there's beer
on their mouths   necks
sunburned   St. Gertrude's holds
my dead family   Pop
took naps with her   liked
to lay his body on her
    her brothers sledge
Pop's stone   drunken swings lop
off his name   my cousins
wipe their palms   they swing
at the iron   climb through
bent bars   the cemetery
calls my father   he will buy
a new stone for Pop
    a custodian hammers back
the bars   rain hits
limestone   layers delaminate
    letters lose their serifs   when
it's time we'll sink
no stone   when he
dies we'll set
my father to ash

FRESHMAN THEOLOGY

newsprint curls out
from corkboard my father opens
a few awning windows
in the empty classroom
he tunes the Four Seasons
falsettos tinny as school band brass
his teenage years rush
over him he hits
the radio off
he will hand out
notebooks for them
to journal feelings
he curates young men
and thinks this atonement

TRESPASS

it's winter your hairs touch
my skin   touch my side
touch the immediate   the bright
burn of it   tread the emptiness
that touches this house   walls
touched with dawn   the late
inside lamp touches windows
breath touches glass   fog touches clear
touch a name   let snow touch cheekbone   it drifts
against fence   touch the latch
touch the gate   the knob   its cool
metal   the hand blooms once
inside   hand that slides open
that turns locks   touch open   touch
young   touch her hair   summer
touches attic dormers   heat pushes
out a fan   so cool in the cellar   the mold
touches stone   sewage rushes in pipes
sounds of the house touch you   touch the half
window   the way out   the awning
hinge   touch the pane touched by slim shoots
touch trim of sky   can you touch
her voice   her full life   her adultness
and you touch her for six months   touch her
around the house   now touch the great
span and for once let her touch a man
let her touch her child   let her
touch herself   her own tall body

Near

as the slow heat leaks
from old panes, when night

makes its shapes, the slatted closet
door strange ribs, when my soft

moon drifts into your hard
pull, our bed holds zephyr

of breath, gather me
as my father would, in the immense

dark I dock my spine
to you

ACKNOWLEDGMENTS

Grateful acknowledgment is made to *The Cortland Review* in which "Cherry Tree" appeared and to Jeffrey Berg for including "Winter Burial" on *jdbrecords*.

I would like to thank David McLoghlin, Rachel Zucker, Yusef Komunyakaa, and Matthew Rohrer for taking in this book, at various stages, and offering encouragement and advice. I am grateful to Alexandra Geis for being a creative compass and a compassionate guide. Thank you to Stephanie Stio at the National Poetry Series, and for his expert stewardship, I am very thankful for David Watson at HarperCollins Publishers.

"A Body Glows Bronze" is after the sculpture *The Age of Bronze (L'Âge d'airain)* by Auguste Rodin, originally titled *The Vanquished (Le Vaincu)*. The model for this work was a twenty-two-year-old Belgian soldier named Auguste Ney.

"Elegy" is dedicated to Tyler Clementi.

"O magnum mysterium" is part of the Latin text of a Christmas choral composition.